Odes *to the* Ordinary

Odes *to the* Ordinary

POEMS

Emily Benson-Scott

GREEN WRITERS PRESS | *Brattleboro, Vermont*

Printed in the United States

10 9 8 7 6 5 4 3 2 1

Green Writers Press is a Vermont-based publisher whose mission is to spread a message of hope and renewal through the words and images we publish. Throughout we will adhere to our commitment to preserving and protecting the natural resources of the earth. To that end, a percentage of our proceeds will be donated to environmental activist groups. Green Writers Press gratefully acknowledges support from individual donors, friends, and readers to help support the environment and our publishing initiative.

Giving Voice to Writers & Artists Who Will Make the World a Better Place

Green Writers Press | Brattleboro, Vermont
www.greenwriterspress.com

ISBN: 979-8-9876631-0-3

COVER & INTERIOR ART:
Ray Scott

THE PAPER USED IN THIS PUBLICATION IS PRODUCED BY MILLS COMMITTED TO RESPONSIBLE AND SUSTAINABLE FORESTRY PRACTICES.

For Robin Ray Scott
My husband, my muse, my heart—
who makes every day into a poem

Contents

VI.
ODES TO STRONG WOMEN

I

*Odes
to Inclement
Weather*

The Problem with Paradise

From Key Largo, we drive down the great white spine
of the Overseas Highway, the ocean a gelatinous expanse
of turquoise, too improbable to be real, lucid and orderly
as an in-ground swimming pool.

Even the pelicans seem disappointed, their long faces exhausted
by so many graceless landings as they fumble through the air
with the disastrous flair
of malfunctioning aircrafts.

Happiness is far more elusive than the easy paradise
promised by couples on honeymoon brochures; it comes in bursts
and flashes, like the nervous dash of a neon green lizard
across a slumbering gray rock

or a two-day train ride back to New York, with nothing but stale bread
and wine to sustain us, necks sore from sleeping in our seats
when I awake to find your black-fabric jacket draped over my curled form
like a cavernous tent of sleep

the vague reminder of your cologne
burrowed deep in the collar,
 the long tunnels of its sleeves,
still lit with fleeting dreams.

Ode to Rain

Underrated, under-appreciated, you've ruined everything from
    weddings to picnics, field trips
and sporting events. No wonder you're always taking the blame.
    Even I hear myself complain
at first, cursing my failure to remember an umbrella on this drizzly
    night, imagining a handful of
dire consequences—from sodden clothes, to bronchitis or a mere
    cold, like someone who's
allowed themselves to grow too old.

But just look how you transform the night—how sidewalks, slick
    with your reflective sheen—
glow red and green, stained with the ink of streetlights. Brake-lights
    too paint the town—
taillights streaking pavement with twin red brushstrokes.
Umbrellas bloom everywhere and the night
is a forest of dark flowers cheerfully pinwheeling on their stems.

I take shelter briefly beneath the aluminum awning of a bodega,
    listening to the rain hammer out
its song overhead, the heavy rhythmic drops on the aluminum
    conjure a calypso concert on a
beach somewhere—a conversation between steel drums. The rain
    pummeling the streets,
running into a gutter below completes the performance, becomes
    uproarious applause, one
standing ovation on top of another.

Continuing my walk home, autumn leaves are rejuvenated by the
    rain, made young again, rinsed
and pressed against the sidewalk, like lily pads leading your eye
    across a pond. They are just the
right distance apart to instill an urge to skip, and as my feet lift from
    the ground, I praise the rain
who rinsed away the years, and for a magical instant made me a
    child again.

Ode to Mud Season

It hardly deserves to be called a season,
this purgatory—lulled between
the dull cold comfort of winter
and the forsythia-yellow mania of spring.

Although it's April in Vermont, the grass is more texture than hue—
more bristle doormat or scrub brush—
bleached and ruined
like the color of absence.

Tiny corpses of last autumn's copper leaves still cling to bare branches
which rattle in the wind like bones in a box.
Pockmarked piles of snow, both disappearing and trenchant
reveal the season's listless indecision.

Residents complain, smother the ground with hay,
hoping to soak up layers of mud,
snowmelt unable to seep through
the still-frozen ground.

Yet there's something full of grace, about this faceless season
the way it refuses to be anything in particular, spared the effort
of strutting out its colors
or promising buoyant balmy nights.

Summer's End

On the Jersey Shore, black-eyed Susans sunk in sand wave against the
    violet-bruised sky
as seagulls exit the scene. The beach, a sly observer of pleasures
    indulged, remains littered with
summer's unserious remnants—wrappers, popsicle sticks, and
    crumpled cans. The sand, eternal,
muddied by evening light, begins to glow bone-white, with fragments
    of shell.

Reeds bow down beneath Fall's encroaching wind, and I run laps
    to remember discipline,
to fit in again, with the rigid world of chairs, hard spines of books, to
    command
students with my ruler-sharp stance, as though my heart had never
    danced with the waves, never yearned
for more—the way contorted pines along the coastal path at Cap
    Martin leaned longingly towards the Mediterranean Sea—
as though I'd never known the sweet collapse of a fresh fig
    on my tongue.

My students will never know the way Summer has undone me,
nearly won me over
to Her permanent ease.

Lake Champlain after a Storm

I crawl out of the cabin of our sailboat astonished
by this dripping silence
the frozen-still surface of the lake, now a thin sheet of glass

reflecting none of the recent trauma, but only
the candy-colored hulls of boats,
the shouldering heft of surrounding mountains.

Surprisingly, the tentative blue sky is brightly unaware of the
        nightmarish storm
just passed, of all that irascible rain, the haranguing waves
that almost sank this brazen craft.

Once again, the world has righted itself, just as this small boat
swerved upright after every bullying gust
and I think, breathing in the sweet newness of the air

it's too easy to forget this lucidity, this moment
when the horizon appears once more, so importantly before you
too easy to give in to the undertow of some private despair

whereas if you just hung on a little longer
you might find, at the other end awaits
this victorious calm, this careful hope.

When It Rains on Your Wedding Day

People sometimes ask about the weather on my wedding day
"It poured," I say, "not a single ray of sunshine, like God was cursing us."
and then I look away.

I tell them how the band sang "Stormy Weather," to make light of things,
as if our marriage would be filled with broken dishes and broken
    promises,
 cheating hearts and multiple miscarriages.

I never tell them how glad I am that it poured on our wedding day
how it reminded me of those long afternoons we used to stay in bed,
    like a pair of invalids
listening to the rain create a soft envelope of sound around us.

how the rain had always seemed a co-conspirator to our love, justifying
    hours of doing nothing
but fooling around under the covers, running the tip of my finger along
    the soft outer edge of your ear
while plotting the hour of our next bubble bath.

I never tell them how the rain always made me feel sheltered, invincible,
    the way I felt when we
exchanged our rings, as though we'd created a safe space for each other,
    where we could whisper
our worst fears and be heard, reveal our impossible dreams and be
    believed.

II

*Odes
to Trees*

Ode to a Quaking Aspen

Because of your petioles, gossamer stalks tapered as blades of grass,
    your vulnerable serrated
heart-shaped leaves spin too easily in the most undetectable breeze.

While surrounding trees disappoint with their listless green leaves,
    yours are perpetually aflutter,
like schoolgirls feverishly exchanging the latest gossip with one
    another.

When the breeze dies a little, your leaves continue to shift and
    shimmer in the sunlit wind like
sequins emblazoned on an evening gown, reflecting the myriad light of
    chandeliers.

When the wind revives, it sets your leaves in motion, your treetop
    buzzing like a hive of bees.
You become densely, intensely alive—now a flock of golden-hued
    migratory butterflies.

When the air is perfectly still, you rest, but then with a single breath,
    your leaves are set a-twirl
like so many whirling dervishes intent on ecstatic union with the
    divine.

Wouldn't it be easier if you felt that breeze less intensely? Like your
    neighbor, that even-keeled
oak with its umbrella of lackadaisical leaves?

Wouldn't it be wise if you harnessed some of your insanity so you
    didn't burn through your
allotted time on earth in a state of uncontrollable mirth—

Although you may never really be at ease, we can all admire how
    alive you seem, always
dancing, quivering, most often with delight, although in darker
    hours with confusion and fright

As the evening fades, your leaves—upturned like an offered
    bouquet—become moon-luminous
in the night, a sole source of light.

Silhouettes

As darkness encroaches, palm fronds—once green and bright, soft and
    nonchalant as a woman's
hair blowing in the breeze—are forced to take up arms, stiffening into
    blades, silhouettes ready
to battle the deepening night.

The canal too seems to be losing the battle against night, blackening
    into invisibility, turning
opaque as an oil slick. Yet, the water in the waning light quivers with
    life—as pelicans, in their
hunt for sustenance, skim low, like so many skipped rocks enlivening
    the surface.

Then there is the tiny elbow moon, its faint light encouraging telephone
    poles to keep their form,
helping them staunchly retain their stiff posture, to shun disappearance.

How valiant are these myriad silhouettes, knowing the futility of the
    fight, how they still resist
being swallowed by the night—at least without one last fleeting grasp
    at light.

Ode to a Red Maple

In autumn, many gather round
to gape at your crimson leaves
certain as blood pumped
through a healthy heart.

Your branches harbor no
premonition of tomorrow,
or the dead cold of winter,
but only radiate the ripest
red mirth.

Some may mourn
the waning days of autumn, the omen
of a single leaf drifting down.

But if this tree were
so outspoken in its beauty
so vibrantly here
every day of the year, would anyone stop to peer?

If we lived more
than our allotted span,
would we burn with such fire?
Such defiance?
Such denial?

III

✿

Odes
to
Abandoned Things

Ode to a Washed-Up Lobster Trap

Even though you're a ghost of your former self, you sit upright,
albeit largely off-center, your sides tilted Tower-of-Pisa-like,
your back slats half missing like a bashed ladder.

Still, you can't complain; you've been rescued, given a second life
as a lawn ornament in someone else's garden.
You've got a great spot to dry out in the sun.

Someone has even tasked you honorably with holding a heavy piece
    of driftwood atop
your sagging upper slats, so you might appear artistic, like a Caryatid
poised and graceful as she endures unthinkable tons of stone atop
    her head.

Think of all the lobsters no longer trapped—think of that redeeming
    fact, how many you've
saved. Yet how you must miss those calm ocean depths, that ready
    sense of purpose, as you sit
useless as a grounded aircraft, inches from the grave.

Ode to the Present Moment

Today, as I wait
for the biopsy results, the world
blindsides me with beauty.

The ordinary eyesore of scaffolding—all that rough blue boarding,
now glows a brilliant heavenly hue—the industrial
tangle of cranes, now soaring graceful birds.

A young couple in the park, eyes moons of adoration,
as they dote under a flowering tree
has all the happiness anyone could ever need.

Why do we want so much?
When everything is right here?
where moist green air wafts warm and cool,

and a young girl blows bubbles,
the soapy splash landing
light and wet against my leg.

Here, where poppy flowers tower, as if to exclaim
I will live brightly and just the way I desire
if only for a short while.

How did I never notice the amber eyes of pigeons,
or come to treasure
the greenish-purple iridescence of their necks?

At the farmer's market, a woman sells challah bread
and even though I have no appetite,
I can't resist the soft pull and tear of the golden-sweet flesh.

I buy a loaf and walk home to wait for the call
as raindrops fall, light and scarce
here and not here, like a dream.

Ode to the Elevated Subway at Night

Gleaming silver centipede, checkered with windows of light,
you weave through the night in wingless flight,
darkness half-concealing the steel undergirding
required to keep you upright.

You're so much lovelier suspended in the air than underground,
    where dark tunnels constrict you,
grip you tightly as a straight-jacket and you shoot joyless, bullet-
    sure to your destination.
Underground, you're as stiff and solemn as figures in a Byzantine
    painting, as if you lacked
joints or muscles, any ability to dance, find joy, or unwind.

But when you're up on those meandering elevated tracks, you have
    your full range of motion back.
You pivot from the waist and swivel from the hips, like an Olympian
    winding up to throw a discus.
You twist like one of Michelangelo's restless nudes, robust with
    musculature, rejoicing
in the possibilities of form. As you glide sinuously through the
    night—more than public transport,
you resemble a carnival ride at Coney Island, seeking to fill your
    passengers with delight.

What to Do with an Ex-Boyfriend's Books

Maybe you wish there had been a prenup, stating that if he tires of you
for no obvious or rational reason, he will hand over all the
    Enlightenment thinkers,
that if he flirts with other women, he must relinquish
the *Dhammapada*, and the *Tao Te Ching*.

But you should have known all along it was temporary,
like the furniture you were storing for a friend who'd gone abroad,
or the one-year lease you signed together
with an option to renew.

You could try and profit from the situation, and sell them used, but
    you can't bear the thought of
seeing those books you know so well—down to every dog-eared
    page—in the hands of another
woman, a mysterious smile on her lips, as she delicately fingers the
    pages of *Faust*, or slides a
bookmark in *The Birth of Tragedy*.

You could deface them, tear out choice passages—the "Fourth Noble
    Truth," so he might never
attain Nirvana. You consider keeping them on your shelves, for him
    to borrow,
available whenever he likes,
a no-strings-attached library.

But you know, of course, the right thing to do is to separate
your books from his, which mingle together on your shelves
like guests at a party, deep in the throes of conversation,
indifferent to the music.

But what about the ones he bought you as gifts, the poetry of Emily
    Dickinson

or the new translation of *Don Quixote*, which you read to one
     another in bed at night before
shutting off the light and leaning your head against his chest, closing
     your eyes in gleeful
surrender, like a child sledding down a short slippery hill.

When it hurts to go near your bookshelves, you realize it's best if
     you send them all
back, so you won't be reminded of him every time you think of
     knights, or windmills,
or solitary women in white. You begin to box them up, planning to
     ship them to the tiny room he
rented on Freeman Street—the cruelty of his new address not lost
     on you—

but then, you wonder, why should you pay for the shipping? You
     kick the boxes outside your
door, write a threatening email, stating he has forty-eight hours
     before you burn them.
You decide you will leave town for those two days, so when you hear
     his footsteps
coming up the stairs, his half-regretful hesitation at your doorstep,
     you will not be tempted

to open the door, and ask if you could borrow Plato's *Symposium* for
     just a little longer—
that in truth, you realized, you hadn't finished with it just yet.

Writer's Block

The mind can be a backyard in winter, buried beneath blankets of
    forgetful white, a place full of frozen
potential, shrubs saddened beneath the burden of snow, forgetting
    the latent inspiration of spring.
You could always just give up . . .

but the neighbor's field, gone to seed will always haunt, with its
    skeleton stalks of corn—shadows
of ideas both rotting and remaining, still
taunting you with their presence

and you decide you really don't want your mind to become
    like that old antique tractor left to rust—
an abandoned sculpture, red slender wheels upturned to the sky—
    a splendid heap,
beautiful and utterly useless.

Ode to a Stripped Bicycle in Brooklyn

This city you've come to call home, has robbed you of everything—
of your wheels—on which you once glided
through its promising streets, feather-light, lively
with hope, oblivious to danger and oncoming cars.

This city has robbed you of all your soft
cushioning, that once protected you from
bumps and surprises, from potholes, accidents
and construction.

This city has robbed you of handlebars and the right
to steer your life in one direction or another
Now, instead of control, there is only   survival.

This city has robbed you of your apple-red shine—
your cannibalized frame pockmarked with age
and rust. It's robbed you of bells and baskets,
every last inch of your glamorous and necessary armor.

This city has robbed you of your fierce potential,
your sleek urgency and power. It's robbed you
of desire, that certain fire that once set you racing
through streets and even up hills.

What's left of you now? What's left
but limping intention, a pale memory of what you set out to do,
a battered triangle,
a sad carcass of your former self.

And yet, you remain!
Faithful, determined and chained, you cling
to this lonely post in the rain, on a deserted block
in your eternal city of dreams.

Ode to Grieving

Surely it's time to move on, but I can't stop remembering
vacations in August, my grandparents greeting us,
their friendly waves and smiles robust with summer's promise.

I still remember the smooth ice-blue vinyl floor of the pool,
where we swam before stepping onto sun-warmed stones.
Sometimes we'd play backgammon, or go for a hike.

Always, after the exertions of a summer's day, we'd retire to the terrace,
the slack contented silence punctuated by the polite swirl of ice-cubes,
demarcating day
from night.

After supper, I'd pretend I was grown-up, sitting at my grandmother's
    dressing table,
lifting the delicate lids off the ceramic chinoiserie, to the fragrant
    surprise
of perfumed powder.

I delighted in the cool clatter of pearls,
their opulent heaviness as I draped them
around my slender neck.

If I liked something, my grandmother insisted
I take it. She had no illusions
about forever.

She made of herself, her heirlooms,
a bridge spanning one generation
to the next.

Tonight, her pearls settle around my collar bone
whispering their soft iridescent promises,
a hopeful future that awaits. . .

But tonight, I'd rather look back, call my mother
who is deep in grief. She can't do her work
or ride her bike along the beach.

All she can do is sit on the floor of her office, her door
closed, her bicycle neglected in the corner,
emails piling up, and tell me about the time

my grandmother came home, radiant
because my grandfather taught her
to whistle through a blade of grass.

Ode to Prisoners in a Park

Three men suited up, unmistakable,
too visible in orange Day-Glo jumpsuits
rake sand to maintain this pristine
seafront park.

One of them leans on his rake to take
in the scene—how it must seem,
the sky exquisite as opium,
yellowing palm fronds swaying
in the tropical breeze—tantalizing
as the hips of a hula dancer.

In an ostentatious display of freedom,
a hawk—jaunty as a kite—glides back and forth
across the wide sky, as he rides
the shifting wind currents.

Another prisoner stares out at the sea with pained
and silent longing. I've come to run here
every day and haven't once taken off my shoes
to feel the cool weight of the waves collapse
against my bare ankles.

IV

🌿

Odes
to
Animals

Flamingos in Flight

Pale pink flamingos wade slow
and listless, almost purposeless
across the salty shallows of the Rhône delta,
hooked necks bowed to the ground
beneath the day's blanketing heat.

With one metamorphic decision towards flight,
they transform into taut arrows of purpose
legs kicked back like a switchblade,
hot pink wings capped with neat black tips
slicing through the stagnant afternoon.

I wish I knew how to choose
from so many dubious options,
take flight in a hot pink blaze
of certainty, soaring off in one direction
across the boundless blue sky.

Day's Catch

On the neighbor's dock, a ghost-white bucket lingers
at the far end, the day's catch left
to putrefy in deadening heat.
When I peer inside, blue crabs sit submerged in warm water
silent, motionless as a stack of plates.

Foolish with hope, I attempt to set them free
into the shallow marsh beneath the suck and release
of the tide. But when I empty out the bucket, the crabs
tumble to the water with sorrowful weight, the tumultuous
stiffness of bodies to a mass grave.

Upside down, their bellies, pillowed with white meat,
glimmer like a heap of diaphanous trash. Alongside them,
beneath the cool water, the living scamper in their sideways ballet,
blue needle-nosed pincers flung open for rough play, claws lit
with the fire of existence, a sudden match-tip redness.

Natal Homing

Sea turtles swept thousands of miles from shore
still manage to navigate their way home, the attraction fierce, magnetic,
steering them back to their place of birth
to forage for food or lay eggs of their own.
Don't we feel that same pull? No matter how far we go? No matter
    how many places we find,
with a better climate, or restaurants, or job prospects?
Isn't there a part of us that simply loves what we know?
no matter how dull or run-down or cold?

Our hearts pine for those old parking lots where we smoked our first
    cigarette,
inhaled that menthol-sharp thrill of rebellion, had our first fumbling
    kiss, gear shift jabbing into
flesh. Our bones ache for those shopping malls where we lied our way
    into R-rated movies,
wasted hours in the cacophonous darkness of arcades.

It's as if the map of that place were imprinted on us, so even if we never
    return,
we spend our lives yearning for some semblance of home,
maybe another small town in some other state,
where we recognize the tired expression of a waitress at a late-night
    diner,

kitchen thick with the smell of grease, the empty streets outside like
    the ones we memorized as
kids—every storefront trashcan and gutter—owning them, by
    knowing them so well, believing
the whole world could be that easy, as soon as we left that nowhere
    place—that would haunt us
for the rest of our days.

Ode to a Purple Gallinule

You dance so lightly over lily pads, gallivanting from one to the next
in search of a meal of insects, without a modicum of doubt or fear,
your orange beak brazen and hopeful as a sunrise, as you pluck
    onward,
your deep rich coat of purple and teal marrying the dusk.

Each lily pad yields, almost sinks beneath the weight of your long
    yellow legs
and oversized feet—large and eccentric, as if two golden Starfish
had latched onto your ankles, as if you had donned fairytale slippers
imbued with magical powers.

Even as these water lilies drift, shift like tectonic plates
forming a precarious surface, you skate across them, unshaken,
as if on solid ice, or terra firma
Always Trusting.

Ode to a Carriage Horse in Central Park

Your leg is restless as a fly, stomping the pavement, as you stand in
    boredom gagging on your bit
that tugs and tears at your petal-soft pink lips, as you wait to haul
    this hearse-like burden.

Stranded in this summer heat, no shade in sight, you stand hemmed
    in by skyscrapers, holy,
forgotten and dwarfed as any church competing with teeming
    industry.

Your blond mane, your ladylike eyelashes, long and curved as the last
    sliver of moon, your regal
nose mapped with auburn and white, are too pretty for this ruthless
    city.

All day, your nostrils breathe fetid air full of fumes and trash.
    Your ears stand erect at the irascible
rush of traffic, the senseless shrieks of horns.

Only your eyes, deep as wounds, are protected by blinders that stifle
    your curiosity as they shield
you from the frightening sight of buses streaming by, fast as bullets
    that nearly graze your hide

as pigeons steal food from your battered bucket and you stand
    straightjacketed by this swirling
confusion, by your harness and your trade—

your hoof engraved with the number 3543, a whip lashing your rear end, forcing your legs,
your aching back to move again. The clownish insult of a feathered purple plume sits atop your head,

lending a festive air that fools so many who fail to see true misery.
When I approach, you look straight at me, a faint plea in the endless liquid

of your eyes, and I sense a glimmer of hope you still hold out for the lavish freedom of open
meadows, for your limbs to dance again.

Element

A seal on a rock is a painful thing to watch,
in spite of his lazing in the sun
and flagrant display of blubber.

When he shinnies across the dry hot stretch of rock
he's like a hostage, hands and feet bound with rope,
forced in quick bursts at the command of his captors.

On land, his flippers are useless as mittens
meant only for scratching or waving hello,
a circus fool employed for the public's amusement.

But slipping back into his element, his familiar silken sphere,
he shoots through the sea with torpedo grace,
becomes pure, fluid belonging—

The way I came home to you last night after another office party,
where they served eighteen-dollar drinks and people talked about
    nothing, as they stared at the
glittering cold perfection of the Manhattan skyline

the way I returned afterwards to our ecstatic routine of frayed red
    tablecloths
toothy white stubs of candles, fat with wax drippings, to the hiss of
    potatoes roasting in the oven,
 the sweet fullness of cheap red wine in my mouth

and to that familiar sea of jazz and conversation when you asked me
    about my day
with genuine curiosity, the warmth from the stove luxurious as fur
    coats around our shoulders.

Ode to an Egret in Central Park

Where on earth did you learn to be so still? In the middle of rush
    hour no less, amidst the
cantankerous complaints of horns, the downtrodden music of hooves
    or self-important strides of passers-by?

Except for two lovers full of awe for the world, the rest are blind to
    the white blade of your
presence, standing serenely in the shallow marsh, as you wait with
    otherworldly patience for your next meal.

You're like a king, lording over the dull green surface of the water,
    now a mirror for your scissor-
sharp reflection, your regal cloak of silky white plumes. It takes a
    certain arrogance, doesn't it? To be so oblivious?

But you've managed to carve out your space, as exact and precise as
    the s-curve of your neck.
You have no doubt about your right to silence, no guilt about cutting
    yourself off from the world.

You understand there's nothing violent about solitude,
that it more closely resembles a merging, the only way to truly escape
    loneliness,
the closest way we come to knowing God.

V

Odes
to
Travel

Motel Six

The cheap nightly rate, copious carafes
of fresh morning coffee, the glassy blue glamour
of an unheated swimming pool
must have been what lured
some restless soul here
dreaming of an existence free as the open road, limitless
as the expanded cable TV
only to find despair
lurking everywhere,
in the clogged drain
and dingy drapes, in the spongy, midnight-blue carpet
steeped in Sin, the broken smoke detector
dangling like an unsightly eye
sprung from its socket, and in futile exertions of an ant
cemented in a stain atop the night stand, struggling with foolish hope
to break free.

After Pompeii

After seeing this naked city of stone
once-elegant villas shot through with weeds
vines worming over time-devoured walls
unsightly as decaying molars,

after the plaster casts of victims,
their final agonies preserved for centuries
hands over mouths, bodies curled and cowering
before the black ocean of volcanic ash

I can hardly wait to get back
to my modest hotel room in Sorrento
listen to the shrill insect whirr of Vespas
from beneath my balcony

or meander through the Monday bustle
of the market, amidst the parakeets and goldfish
the summer-full bins of eggplant
obscenely oversized mounds of black olives stuffed in cellophane

Then stroll down the side streets, full of awe at the unruly Bougainvillea
with its imperial desire to conquer
spilling hot pink down every white-washed wall

And then at night to smell to the strangely reassuring, smoke-singed
     summer air
as the citizens of Sorrento start controlled fires to burn their daily trash—
flames purifying odors to a clean woodsy scent
like the breath of normalcy.

Pilgrimage

The room where Keats died is more holy than a church
with far fewer sinful acquisitions--none of the gold and marble
that lavishly adorn the Vatican--where I had just been forced
in the deadening heat of August, to don a sweater and cover my bare
    shoulders.

In the room where Keats died, there are no pantheon-sized domes
or streams of celestial light—only a narrow bed,
a sliver of a desk beneath the large window,
flanked by the kind of shutters that fly open to life.

Where Keats found himself with fading hopes of staying alive,
there were no frescoes full of angels and trumpets, depicting the glories
of a distant heavenly realm. There was only a place
    for him to write.

Had he lived past twenty-five, I imagine him at this desk,
aching to describe the ordinary majesty, the sorely tangible beauty
of this world before him--where couples embrace now on the Spanish
    Steps and
children splash in Bernini's fountain, *The Sinking Boat.*

When I leave his room, I do something I've never done, stand in the
    middle of a fountain,
cup my hands, and wet down my hair, feet planted firmly in *The Sinking
    Boat* as water drips
down the long yellow tendrils of my hair, drops landing, one by one
on my shamefully bare shoulders.

Ode to a Souvenir

How foolish it seemed at the time, to stuff in my suitcase this delicate
    goblet salvaged from a wine tasting
in the Loire Valley. It would surely shatter before I returned home,
    and still I shepherded
the fragile chalice through airports—shrouded in fabrics,
    as though it were a saintly relic.
And then I forgot all about it.

Until last night, when fishing in the dark recesses of my cabinets for
    an extra cup, I came across the familiar goblet
embossed with the faded remnants of the word—Cheverny—and
    then what an enormous flood
of memories poured forth from that paltry container, as if it were large
    as an amphora, limitless
as Amalthea's Horn.

As I turned the glass in my hand, like a crystal ball in reverse, that
    afternoon at Château de Cheverny
sped back to me with alarming clarity—the five o'clock
    feeding of a hundred foxhounds—
a calicoed mass of quivering anticipation as they exploded through
    the gate in a waterfall rush
of barking, their hunger naked and boundless as our frantic
    exploration.

I sometimes wondered why we went through all the logistical duress,
    the enormous expense
of those summer-long travels, just to see some castles and drink fine
    wine?
And yet, how grateful I was for that simple glass, which brought me
    hurtling back to that halcyon afternoon, when we were perhaps
more alive—a day, Risen, miraculous from the close-lipped
    graveyard of the past.

Ode to a Stranger on a Plane

On the flight home from Iceland, a radiant stranger
sat beside me, petite, self-contained, but sociable,
the way you'd hope any passenger would be
not too garrulous as to mute your own agenda for the ride,
but not too oblivious as to make you feel an unbearable divide.

In the span of an hour, I learned she lived in Woodstock,
got divorced years ago, then retired, went on to pursue
her photography and spiritual path. She even told me how she lied
to get her first job working for a newspaper and how she adopted
a three-legged cat she'd found in an abandoned lot.

I told her as much, if not more—my disappointments,
and battles, things I couldn't even explore in this poem.
I wondered why this rarely happened in a grocery store,
or a laundromat, given the long wait, and the mesmerizing
effect of the spin cycle.

Although I had only known this woman
for an hour or two, I knew that if the captain
were to make a troubling announcement, I would clasp
this angel-stranger's hand and somehow manage
to transcend the fiery descent.

Reykjavik

At the end of my fifth summer overseas
my mother surprised me and flew
with her best friend to Reykjavik.

What startled me was the supreme
spontaneity of her gesture—my mother who
had always kept me tethered to this earth

as if her hand forever clutched a slender string
attached to a helium balloon that tugged continuously
upwards, towards the forgetful sky.

Here she was in Iceland, joining me up in the clouds—my mother
who had saved me from heartbreak, illness and financial ruin,
who did all that she could, even if I remained largely misunderstood.

Or so I thought until I saw her there in Reykjavik, standing before
the impossibly tall church, her eyes lit with a certain fire. It seemed
for once, I'd taught her a little something about how to live.

A Tour of Dove Cottage

I did not care to hear about the *houseplace*, such a Germanic and
  forthright phrase—
the busiest room of the house we were told, where the Wordsworths
  ate supper
and performed chores, like cooking on the fire, poor William caught
  in this quagmire
of daily deeds—weeds in the otherwise well-tilled garden of his verse.

I certainly didn't care to know of the coal-hole under the stairs
that would have been used to store wood and peat
or the pantry for storing flour jam and wheat
(As if a poet should need to eat!)
Even the double washstand, the rarest of antiques, failed to impress
probably added to my distress—a lake poet at least might have bathed
in the lake on a hot summer's day, his head abuzz with verse,
while sunbathers lay listless on the shore,
content in their thoughtless summer slumber.

Upon hearing news that the Wordsworths entertained in the upstairs
sitting room, since it was more brightly lit— I found myself wandering
into William's bedroom where I imagined he peered
through the curtains each night to watch the moon glittering
      on the lake.

The guide ushered us to the final masterpiece, the surprisingly petite
sofa where Wordsworth composed his poems while in the bliss
of solitude. Were we to believe, his soul might still be resting here
on this hallowed divan?

Instead, my mind wandered to his daffodils,
ten thousand dancing in the breeze,
where his eternal spirit seemed more likely to reside
in those very lines—his best victory over time.

Leaving the City in Spring

Streets rush by, gray and sad, spring still smothered
but for the occasional burst of color--the daffodil yellow
of a cab, the racy harlot red of a streetlight.
Skyscrapers shrink in the distance, and the sky, losing its shyness
takes over. Trees, messy and abundant as weeds, cast shadows
long as buildings. Ponds, nature-made, and arbitrarily placed, grace
the landscape with their still faces. White breasts of geese,
tiny wind-bloated sails, glide over the surface of the water and
everywhere spring ruptures the stillness of the landscape,
breathes through everything.

Ode to Niagara Falls

I want to live like this
with the blustering rush of waterfalls
the mindless certainty of rivers traveling
towards the sea's infinity
I want to be full of the same sound and
fury, signifying nothing, except rage
against the dying of the light.
I want to live with the same heedless
purpose, every moment full of
tumultuous passion, for the smallest things--
maraschino cherries, a midnight stroll.
I want to live like this, in a miasma of
mist, an ether of dreams
where rainbows are predictable and trenchant
as the day, where the white winks of birds rise
like the angels of free spirits from this low heaven
where wave after wave of water
hurtles over this cliff of rock
like a school of dolphins
 plunging into an uncertain
Abyss
where there is nothing
And also

Everything.

VI

✻

*Odes
to
Strong Women*

Ode to a Topless Woman in France

On the beach, French women go topless,
mothers and grandmothers alike—tan breasts pendulous and
    mammalian
 alongside the pert invitation of young nipples

It happens even on balconies where across from our Airbnb
a woman emerges each morning
to water the plants without a shred of clothing or shame

Graceful, on tiptoe, as if attired for an elegant ball,
she lifts her watering can, sprinkles her petunias,
nourishing their sumptuous magenta spill down the side of her balcony.

One might expect this from a starlet,
a Fellini-esque goddess or Narcissus.
But by conventional standards, she is no beauty.

Short and rotund, her breasts are small and uneven in size.
Her buttocks sag, and her legs are stocky.
Her hair is cut off bluntly at her shoulders.

Inclined to do what she pleases, she's like a queen
of an exotic island nation greeting sailors or missionaries—
feeling not shame or fear, but only

the sun's warmth dance across her body's topography,
every bulge and fold of flesh
as deserving as the earth.

In the Company of Writers

When your best friend gives birth for the third time,
and you imagine her radiant with sweat,
a tiny universe swaddled in her arms,
just as you've lost your second goldfish due to sheer neglect,

think of Colette at fifty, learning to ski, the racy thrill
of plunging down a mountain, the soft reassurance of snow,
her twenty-year-old-lover in tow,
impressionable as the new white powder.

When you'd do anything not to spend another night
alone, even date a much older man, while he drones on
about his Arabian horses, remember Proust, writing
in the forgiving ocean of his bed, buoyed up on pillows

safe in his cork-lined room, heavy velvet drapes keeping out the
    world so
he might know better, the one inside, like traveling to the interior
of a country—a dense rain forest where thoughts emerge as bright
    surprises, exotic
as an emerald parrot, or a red hibiscus with its trumpeting
    insistence.

Listen to Virginia Woolf and rent a room of your own,
where the day stretches out before you, a meandering sunlit path,
the sky above, a guileless robin's egg blue, as if the world were newly
hatched, and you could hold it in your arms.

Ode to a Single Mom

My friend adopted a baby by herself,
said she was sick of waiting around for Mr. Right.
And besides,
she was running out of time.

So she turned her office into a nursery, painted the walls a soft mint green
bought curtains and baby blankets to match,
with a jungle theme, a plush emerald green carpet,
his room lush and mysterious as a rainforest.

And when he finally arrived, his Cheerio-sized mouth,
his tiny simian hands and feet blindly grasping, for food, then air,
his mother hardly had time to sleep let alone
tend to anyone else's needs.

And now, seeing them together, her eyes wide as moons
as she lies on her back holding him over her
his arms propped out like the wings of a plane—
it seems she has finally found Mr. Right.

House Husband

Schooldays, when I came home, you were always there, the smell
    of freshly baked bread
warming the kitchen, one loaf in the oven, another rising. I loved
    watching you lift
the old striped cloth, revealing the dough doubling, but sometimes
    I winced
when you wiped your hands on your red apron, that scarlet
    embarrassment,
that set you apart from so many other fathers.

Winter mornings, I'd watch you heroically shovel the drive, strong
    arms heaving wet snow aside,
my mother waving goodbye as she left for work, my eyes focusing
    on the telltale sliver of red
beneath the workmanlike coat, the heavy down parka making you
    seem more handsome,
even masculine, if it weren't for the hem of that ever-present apron.

In the evenings you read books—natural history, science,
    philosophy—the ones you never
finished in college, books you would give me over the years,
    nourishing as the meals you
prepared for decades, the vitamins you mailed to me in college
    where I went to study and
become more than what the world believed I was destined for—

a woman waiting for a man, a hot meal on the stove as her husband
    collapsed,
gratified from a hard day's work, a woman who disappeared politely
    to tuck the children into bed
and clean the kitchen, drying chapped hands on her worn
    red apron.

Ode to Françoise Gilot

Out of all his lovers, you were the only one who walked.
You were no Marie-Thérese, naïve and sunny enough
to be painted in yellow, but who, after a brush with Picasso,
a lifetime of waiting to be properly wed,
hung herself in a garage in the South of France.

You were no Dora Maar, dark and weepy,
face depicted in shards of sadness, tears that burned
through to the bone. On the terrace of a Parisian café
Dora demonstrated with a knife trick, a pair
of bloody gloves, her capacity for self-mutilation.

You always had an instinct for self-preservation,
a penchant for flight. Your work is full of soaring
possibility—French doors opening onto balconies
flooded with sea and sky. Even your abstractions
of birds seemed real to Matisse.

Sometimes, I imagine you in your studio,
surrounded by your white paintings, each one
blank and hopeful as a new beginning.

Ode to a Late Bloomer

On the rosebush, flowers flaunt
their meteoric beauty like debutantes
in velvet dresses, oiled with perfume.

But one bud prefers not to bloom.
Imagine the angry relatives, their frustration
with her refusal to join the rest.

She clearly prefers the tight-fisted
promise of potential, the succulent
secrecy of her budded vessel

to the ready success of her sisters
—beauty queens hoping to impress
some nebulous panel of judges.

Each will fade to an elder rose past her prime
their fragrant beauty collapsed,
breasts a nest for suckling bees.

She prefers airy hope and the perfected
cities of her dreams to the finality
of having her feet squarely planted in reality.

Acknowledgments

The author wishes to thank the community at Battenkill Books, especially Connie Brooks, for her support and introduction to the many wonderful books published by Green Writers Press. The author also wishes to thank the editors of the following journals and anthologies in which the following poems first appeared, sometimes in slightly different form:

Southern Poetry Review: "Motel Six"

Nimrod International Journal of Poetry and Prose: "The Problem with Paradise," and "Day's Catch"

Atlanta Review: "Pilgrimage"

Blue Stocking Society: "What to Do with an Ex-Boyfriend's Books"

Cold Mountain Review: "Flamingos in Flight"

Green Hills Literary Lantern: "Here" (Now "Ode to the Present Moment")

Jewish Currents: "Writer's Block"

From the Finger Lakes: A Poetry Anthology: "The Problem with Paradise"

Poem Bouquet: "Motel Six"

The author also wishes to thank the following for their ongoing support:

Lynne Potts, former poetry editor at *AGNI*, and Andrea Fleck Clardy, dear friend and playwright, both of whom read and generously edited many early drafts of unpublished poems; Dede Cummings and the wonderful staff at Green Writers Press; Billy Collins, former U.S. Poet Laureate, for reading my poems early on and urging me to submit; my students at LaGuardia Community College for helping me to understand what makes a good poem; fellow poet Sarah Markgraf, Professor at Bergen Community College, for her steady encouragement; Katia Ustinova for her unflagging enthusiasm; Dean Benson for passing on his infectious love of literature; Frances Benson for her constant support, editing, and especially her publishing expertise; Mary Rita Scott for her advice on covers, titles, and book design; the late Ray Scott for his paintings, some of which grace the cover and the pages of this book, and for always believing in me. I am also grateful to my loving husband and muse, Robin Ray Scott, for cherishing my work and providing constant sources of inspiration for poems as we explore the world together.

About the Author

AUTHOR PHOTO © JORGE COLOMBO

EMILY BENSON-SCOTT's work has appeared in *Southern Poetry Review, Colorado Review, Atlanta Review, Green Hills Literary Lantern, Nimrod International Journal,* and *Cold Mountain Review,* among other journals. Her travel writing has appeared in *London Daily Telegraph, Time Out New York, Delta Sky, Venice, Postcards Magazine,* and *Ultratravel.* She holds a BA in international relations from Cornell University and an MFA in creative writing from Goddard College. Formerly an adjunct professor for CUNY colleges in NYC, for the last decade she and her husband have worked remotely from locations around the globe, including Iceland, Norway, Ireland, England, Scotland, France, Italy and the Greek Isles, among other countries.

More can be found at: www.emilybensonscott.com

9 798987 663103